250+
PICK-UP LINES

A Collection of 250+ Funny, Cheesy, Corny, Sweet, Romantic, Flattering and Hilarious Pickup Lines

by Love Guru

Published by:

Love Guru

© Copyright 2014 – Love Guru

ISBN-13: 978-1505806311
ISBN-10: 1505806313

Table of Contents

Introduction

Enjoy these Awesome Pick-Up Lines. Some are Old... Some are New... But all of them are Awesome... They might either get you the Girl or get you Slapped by the Girl... On the brighter side you get to touch the girl :P ;)... So use your brains before trying these pick-up lines...

I have divided these pick-up lines into different sections. It was difficult to distinguish the categories for some of them so you might find the same pick-up line in more than one section or in a wrong section 'according to you'. I recommend you to simply enjoy them and try some of them if you get a chance. Have FUN!!!

Funny Pick Up lines

1. Did you fart, 'cause you just blew me away."

2. Do you know karate? 'Cause your body is really kickin'.

3. Apart from being sexy, what do you do for a living?

4. Can I have directions? ["To where?"] To your heart.

5. Baby, somebody better call God because HE's missing an angel!

6. Can I get your picture to prove to all my friends that angels really do exist?

7. Did the sun come out or did you just smile at me?

8. Baby, you must be a broom, bcoz you just swept me off my feet.

9. Do you have the time? [Gives the time] No, the time to write down my number?

10. Hi, the voices in my head told me to come over and talk to you.

11. Are your feet tired? 'cuz you've been running through my mind all day.

12. Do you have a band aid? I hurt my knee when I fell for you.

13. Do you work for NASA? Because you're out of this world.

14. See my friend over there? He wants to know if you think I'm cute.

15. Hi, did your license get suspended for driving all these guys crazy?

16. I'm invisible. (Really?) Can you see me? (Yes) How about tomorrow night?

17. Are you a magnet? Because I'm attracted to you..."

18. Beww BEWWW Beww (What?) That is the sound of the ambulance coming to pick me up because when I saw you my heart stopped!

19. Is your name Summer? 'Cause you are HOT!

20. Damn, I'm glad I'm not blind!

21. I would say God bless you but it looks like he already did.

22. Remember me? Oh, that's right, i've met you only in my dreams.

23. Excuse me; I think you owe me a drink." [She says, "Why?"] "Because when I saw you from across the room I dropped mine. It was a rum and Coke, and I'm [your name].

24. My love for you is like diarrhea, I just can't hold it in."

25. (Look at his / her shirt label) When they say, "What are you doing?" You say, "Checking to see if you were made in heaven."

26. Are you a magnet? Cuz I m attracted to you

27. Roses are red, violets are blue, how would you like it if I came home with you?

28. "If a thousand painters worked for a thousand years, they could not create a work of art as beautiful as you."

29. Are you a parking ticket? (What?) You got fine written all over you."

30. You must be the cause of global warming because you're hot!"

31. "I think I must be dying because I'm looking at Heaven."

32. "My love for you is like the energizer bunny; it keeps going and going."

33. Baby, you're like a student and I am like a math book, you solve all my problems."

34. I'm new in town. Could you give me directions to your apartment?

35. "Hey you know Dr. Phil says I am afraid of commitment....Do you want to prove him wrong?"

Your lips look lonely. Would they like to meet mine?

Romantic Pick Up Lines

1. Do you believe in love at first sight or do I need to walk by again?

2. Do you have a map? I just keep on getting lost in your eyes

3. Did it hurt? When you fell from heaven.

4. There's so much to say but your eyes keep interrupting me.

you wanna know whats the best thing in my life?
It's the first word of this sentence ;)

5. If I could rearrange the alphabets, I'd put U and I together.

6. You can't be real. May I pinch you to see if I'm dreaming?

7. I have never had a dream come true until the day that I met you.

8. If you were a tear in my eye, I wouldn't cry for fear of losing you.

9. So how was heaven when you left?"

10. You must be the cause of global warming because your hot!"

11. Can I take a picture of you, so I can show Santa my wish for Christmas?

12. Wouldn't we look cute on a wedding cake together?"

13. "If a thousand painters worked for a thousand years, they could not create a work of art as beautiful as you."

I'm no organ donor but I'd be happy to give you my heart.

14. I feel like Richard Gere, I'm standing next to you, the Pretty Woman."

15. You're so beautiful that you made me forget my pickup line.

16. "I think God took the color from the ocean and put it in your eyes.

17. Can I get your picture to prove to all my friends that angels really do exist?"

18. Hello. Cupid called. He says to tell you that he needs my heart back."

19. "I think I must be dying because I'm looking at Heaven."

20. You must be in a wrong place – the Miss Universe contest is over there."

21. There's only one thing I want to change about you and that's your last name.

you take
my breath away!!

Cheesy Pick Up Lines

1. Hey, my name's Microsoft. Can I crash at your place tonight??

2. "Do you like raisins? How do you feel about a date?"

3. Damn, if being sexy was a crime, you'd be guilty as charged!

4. "Feel my shirt. Know what it's made of? Boyfriend material."

I lost my teddy bear, can I sleep with you?

5. Can you touch me so I can tell my friend's I've been touched by an angel.

6. Do you have a map? I just keep on getting lost in your eyes

7. Does your dad own a dairy company, 'cause you've got a nice set of jugs.

8. Hello, I'm a thief, and I'm here to steal your heart.

9. Do you work at McDonalds? Cuz I want u to be in my happy-meal!

10. Do you come with coffee and cream, cuz ur my sugar!

11. Did u just come out of the oven, cuz u r hot!

12. Stand still so I can pick you up!

13. If I had a nickel every time I saw someone as beautiful as you, then I'd have five cents.

14. If you were a chicken, you'd be impeccable." Granted!

15. there are many fish in the sea but you're the only one that's caught my eye

16. "Well, here I am. What are your other two wishes?"

17. "Did your license get suspended for driving all these guys crazy?"

18. "Know what's on the menu? Me 'n' u."

19. It's a good thing I have my library card, because I am totally checking you out."

20. I was blinded by your beauty; I'm going to need your name and phone number for insurance purposes."

21. Excuse me, I think you have something in your eye. Nope, it's just a sparkle.

22. There's only one thing I want to change about you and that's your last name

23. I think I was blind before I met you

24. I know somebody who likes you but if I weren't so shy, I'd tell you who...

Hey girl, feel my sweater. You know what it's made of? Boyfriend material.

25. Do you know karate? Cause your body's kickin!

26. What do you like to do for fun, cuz I'm gonna ask you out...

27. Life without you is like a broken pencil...pointless.

28. Something's wrong with my eyes, because I can't take them off you."

29. You're so sweet, you're giving me a toothache."

30. Something is wrong with my cell phone...its just that your numbers not in it.

31. I bet you need a map to find out how far those legs go up.

32. I hope there's a fireman around, cause you're smokin'!

33. There aren't enough "O"'s in the word "smooth" to describe how smooth you are.

34. I lost my teddy bear can I sleep with you.

35. Honey, you give new meaning to the definition of 'edible'.

Flattering Pick Up Lines

1. If you were a laser, would you be set on stunning?
2. I bet the sun rises just to see you smile.
3. Hey, weren't you Miss Texas (or state of your choice).
4. If I were a judge in a pageant, you'd get my vote.
5. I've had a really bad day today but it always makes me feel better when I see a pretty girl smile. Would you smile for me?
6. They say that milk does the body good and you are definitely proof of that.
7. If anyone should faint, please don't stand over them. Otherwise they will think you are an angel and they have died and gone to heaven.
8. I am not really a heavy drinker but being around you is intoxicating.
9. If this place is a steak house, you must be the prime rib.
10. Is it hot in here or is it just you?
11. I bet there are plastic surgeons who can't get legs to look that good.

12. What do you do for a living besides getting all the guys to fall in love with you?

13. Your father must have been royalty to make a princess like you.

14. I bet the wind blows just to feel how gorgeous your hair is.

15. If your father was Chuck Norris, I'd still ask you out on a date.

16. Have you ever been arrested? Because it has to be illegal to look that good.

If you stood in front of a mirror and held up 11 roses, you would see 12 of the most beautiful things in the world.

17. I never believed in heaven until I saw you.

18. I bet all the goddesses of love and beauty write to you for advice.

19. Of all the paintings and artwork ever done of beautiful women, they all fall short of you.

20. You know, you might be asked to leave soon. You are making the other women look really bad.

21. Have they ever named a hurricane after you? Because you are definitely blowing me away.

22. Your father must have been an alien because there is nothing else like you on this earth.

23. Does the ocean sigh in relief when you go for a swim?

24. You know, artists have tried for centuries to capture the beauty that you possess.

25. You can never take a trip to Alaska. (When they ask "Why?") Because you would melt all the ice.

26. I thought diamonds were the most beautiful thing until I laid eyes on you.

27. They must have been crazy to let an angel as beautiful as you out of heaven.

28. I thought I saw two sapphires sparkling from across the room. Then I realized it was your eyes.

29. I was wondering if you had a moment to spare for me to admire you up close.

30. If your eyes were the ocean, I'd be lost at sea right now.

31. Excuse me, I am looking for directions to the quickest way to your heart.

32. I like a woman who looks like an angel but has a little bit of the devil in her eyes.

33. So you must be the reason men fall in love.

34. When you step outside, I bet the flowers bloom just for you.

35. If you were a teardrop, I'd never cry for fear of losing you.

36. If you are as beautiful on the inside as you are the outside, then your soul must be stunning.

37. I have never seen that exact color anywhere else except your eyes.

38. If you are as intelligent as you are beautiful then you must be a rocket scientist.

39. If I had a rose for every time I met someone as beautiful as you, I'd have only one rose.

40. Whenever I think of the finer things in life, I think of expensive cars, fine wine…and you.

41. Girl, you got more curves than a race track.

Pick Up Lines for Starting Chat

1. Aside from being sexy, what do you do for a living?

2. If I could rearrange the alphabet, I'd put 'I' and 'U' together.

3. Do you believe in love at first sight—or should I walk by again?

4. Feel my shirt. Know what it's made of? Boyfriend material

5. Well, here I am. What are your other two wishes?

6. Did your license get suspended for driving all these guys crazy?

7. Baby, if you were words on a page, you'd be fine print.

8. Did you just come out of the oven? Because you're hot.

9. Life without you is like a broken pencil...pointless.

10. Something's wrong with my eyes, because I can't take them off you.

11. You're so sweet; you're giving me a toothache.

12. Hi, I am (mention your name), what is yours?
(requires 100% confidence)

13. . Turn to the girl sitting next to you at the bar and
say... "I'm not really this tall....I'm sitting on my
wallet."

14. This one was uttered by Clark Gable in 'Red
Dust" in 1932. "Mind if I get drunk with you?"

15. "If you were a fruit, you'd be a fineapple." ...and
along the same produce lines... "If you were a
vegetable, you'd be a cutecumber."

16. "Is your name homework? 'Cause I'm not doing
you but I should be."

I would offer you a cigarette, but you're already smoking hot.

17. "Can I follow you home? Cause my parents
always told me to follow my dreams."

18. "Do you have any raisins?" (No) "Well how
about a date?"

19. "On a scale from 1 to America, how free are you tonight?"

20. . "Can i take a picture of you so I can show Santa Clause what I want for Christmas?"

21. "You're hot. I'm ugly. Let's make average babies."

22. . "Are you from Tennessee? Because you're the only 10-I-see!"

23. "I would flirt with you, but I'd rather seduce you with my awkwardness."

24. "If you were a potato, you'd be a really nice potato."

25. "Is your name wifi? Cuz I think I can feel a connection here."

26. "Giant polar bear (What?) It's an icebreaker. Hi, my name is…."

27. "Do you have sunburn, or are you always this hot?"

28. "Hey I just realized this, but you look a lot like my next girlfriend."

29. "Life without you would be like a broken pencil…pointless."

30. "You look life my first wife! (How many have you had?) None."

31. "Rejection can lead to emotional stress for both parties involved and emotional stress can lead to physical complications such as headaches, ulcers, cancerous tumours, and even death! So for my health and yours, JUST SAY YES!"

Sweet pickup line

1. You're eyes are bluer than the Atlantic Ocean and baby, I'm all lost at sea.

2. Do you have a pencil? Cause I want to erase your past and write our future.

3. How was Heaven when you left it?

4. You are so beautiful that you give the sun a reason to shine.

5. The only thing your eyes haven't told me is your name.

6. I think I can die happy now, coz I've just seen a piece of heaven.

7. You must be a magician, because every time I look at you, everyone else disappears. I'm no organ donor, but I'd be happy to give you my heart.

8. When I first saw you I looked for a signature, because every masterpiece has one.

9. Excuse me...Hi, I'm writing an essay on the finer things in life, and I was wondering if I could interview you.

10. Has anyone ever told you that your eyes are clear like the ocean? Because I can see straight into your soul.

11. If I had a rose for every time I thought of you, I would be walking through my garden forever.

12. I wish I was one of your tears, so I could be born in your eyes, run down your cheek, and die on your lips.

13. Can you give me directions to your heart? I've seemed to have lost myself in your eyes.

14. It's not my fault I fell in love. You are the one that tripped me.

Are you going to kiss me or am I going to have to lie to my journal?

15. God gave us two ears, two eyes, two legs and two hands, but he only gave us one heart, and he wanted me to find you and tell you, you are the second one

16. This morning I saw a flower and I thought it was the most beautiful thing I have ever seen; until I met you..

17. Was your father a thief? 'Cause someone stole the stars from the sky and put them in your eyes.

18. I thought happiness started with an H. Why does mine start with U?

19. What time do you have to be back in heaven?

20. "When I'm older looking back at all of my finest memories, and I'll think of the day my children were born, the day I got married, and the day that I met you. "

21. If you wake up in a RED room, with no windows or doors..don't be alarmed, baby girl…you're just in my heart

22. Your earrings are the mirrors which reflect the moonlight into your eyes

23. Girl, you're really good at this catch and release thing. Every time I catch my breath around you, you make me lose it again.

24. I think you've got something in your eye. Oh never mind, it's just a sparkle.

25. Do you know what I did last night? I looked up at the stars, and matched each one with a reason why I love you.

26. I play the field, and it looks like I just hit a home run with you.

27. If a star fell for every time I thought of you, the sky would be empty.

28. When I first saw you I looked for a signature, because every masterpiece has one.

29. Would you touch me so I can tell my friends I've been touched by an angel?

30. If I had to choose between breathing and loving you.... I'd take my last breath to say "I Love You"

31. Your smile lit up the room so I had to come over."

32. Hi, my friend thinks you're kinda cute, but I don't. I think you're absolutely gorgeous.

33. Are You Blood, Cause My Heart Cant Survive Without You

34. I was gonna say something really sweet about you but when I saw you I was speechless.

35. We must be near an airport, because my heart just took off when I saw you!

36. Your eyes are as blue as the sea after a storm

37. Because of you, I laugh a little harder, cry a little less, and smile a lot more.

38. If I walked a millimetre for every time I thought of you, I would have walked across the Earth a million times

39. (On a rainy day) I figured out why the sky was grey today...all the blue is in your eyes.

40. If you know a person's name: "Hi, [name]." How did you know my name? "Isn't every beautiful girl named that?"

41. Are you a girl scout because you tie my heart in knots.

42. (give a dozen plastic roses) "I'll stop loving you, when these roses die.

43. May I have the distinguished honour and privilege of sitting next to you?

44. "If kisses were snowflakes, I'd send you a blizzard."

45. You look like the morning sun after a long night of darkness.

46. This morning I saw a beautiful flower...and thought of you.

47. Wouldn't we look cute on a wedding cake together?

48. If I had a dollar for every time I thought of you, I'd only have a dollar because you never leave my mind.

49. You stole my heart, so can I steal your last name?

50. If beauty were time, you'd be an eternity.

51. Excuse me, can you empty your pockets? I believe you have stolen my heart.

Can I borrow a kiss? I promise I'll give it back.

52. You're so sweet, your giving me cavities

53. the only crime i will ever commit is stealing your heart

54. If I was your heart would you let me beat?

55. I now believe in Angels. Do you believe in fate?

56. If you had eleven roses and you looked in the mirror; then you'd see twelve of the most beautiful things in the world.

57. How does it feel? she asks what; you say 2 be the only star in the sky

58. It took 3 tries to approach you. I kept loosing my breath ...

59. You: Can I borrow a quarter? She: why? (if she says sure or something else get her to ask you why) You: so I can call my mom and tell her I just met the girl of my dreams. (have something prepared to quickly follow through)

60. My life is so sad and lonely (why) because your not in it

61. Hey baby do you like a man that can carry big things because I have the biggest sweetheart

62. I'll put a tear drop in the ocean. When you find it is when I'll stop loving you.

Top 30 Pick Up Lines

1. "If I were a stop light, I'd turn red every time you passed by, just so I could stare at you a bit longer."

2. "I was so enchanted by you that I ran into that wall over there. So I am going to need your name and number for insurance purposes."

3. "For a moment I thought I'd died and gone to heaven. Now I see that I am very much alive, and heaven has been brought to me."

4. "If I were to ask you out on a date, would your answer be the same as the answer to this question?"

5. "Do you have a Band-Aid? I just scraped my knee falling for you."

6. "You're so beautiful that you made me forget my pickup line."

7. "There's something wrong with my cell phone. It doesn't have your number in it."

8. "Is there an airport nearby or is that just my heart taking off?"

9. "If I had a star for every time you brightened my day, I'd have a galaxy in my hand."

10. "Would you grab my arm? I want to tell my friends I've been touched by an angel."

11. "I must be a snowflake, because I've fallen for you."

12. "I think there's something wrong with my eyes...I can't take them off of you."

13. "Hey, how are you? [Fine] Wait, I didn't ask how you looked!"

14. "Be unique and different, say yes."

15. "Do you believe in love at first sight, or should I walk by again?"

16. "Excuse me, I think you have something in your eye. Oh wait, it's just a sparkle."

17. "Hello. Cupid called. He says to tell you that he needs my heart back."

18. "You see my friend over there? [Point to friend] He wants to know if YOU think I'M cute."

19. "[Extending hand] Would you hold this for me while I go for a walk?"

20. "I was gonna say something really sweet about you but when I saw you I was speechless. "

21. My life is so sad and lonely (why) because you're not in it.

22. It took 3 tries to approach you. I kept loosing my breath ...

23. "You look cold. Want to use me as a blanket?"

24. "Hey, baby, you're so fine you make me stutter. Wha-wha-what's your name?"

25. "[As she's leaving] Hey, aren't you forgetting something? [What?] ME!!"

26. If you wake up in a RED room, with no windows or doors..don't be alarmed, baby girl...you're just in my heart

27. I now believe in Angels. Do you believe in fate?

28. "I don't have a library card, do you mind if I check you out?"

29. "Do you have a twin? Then you must be the most beautiful girl in the world!"

30. "Rejection can lead to emotional stress for both parties involved and emotional stress can lead to physical complications such as headaches, ulcers,

cancerous tumours, and even death! So for my health and yours, JUST SAY YES!"

Printed in Great Britain
by Amazon